AF480551

Hex codes, or hexadecimal codes, are a way to represent colors in digital devices and web design. Each hex code refers to a very specific color. A hex color is expressed as a six-digit combination of numbers and letters, preceded by a pound sign or hashtag, defined by its mix of red, green, and blue (RGB). The first two letters or numbers refer to red, the next two refer to green, and the last two refer to blue.

The color values are defined as values between 00 and FF. Hex codes are a universal way to describe colors. This book is specifically about shades of black.

A is for arsenic

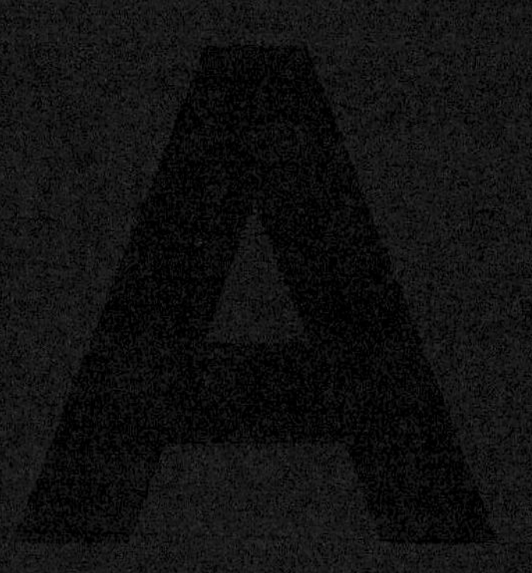

#21272B

a is for asphalt

a

#080202

D is for dark gunmetal

#1F262A

d is for diesel

d

#130000

E is for ebony

E

40CORD

e is for eerie black

e

f is for foundry

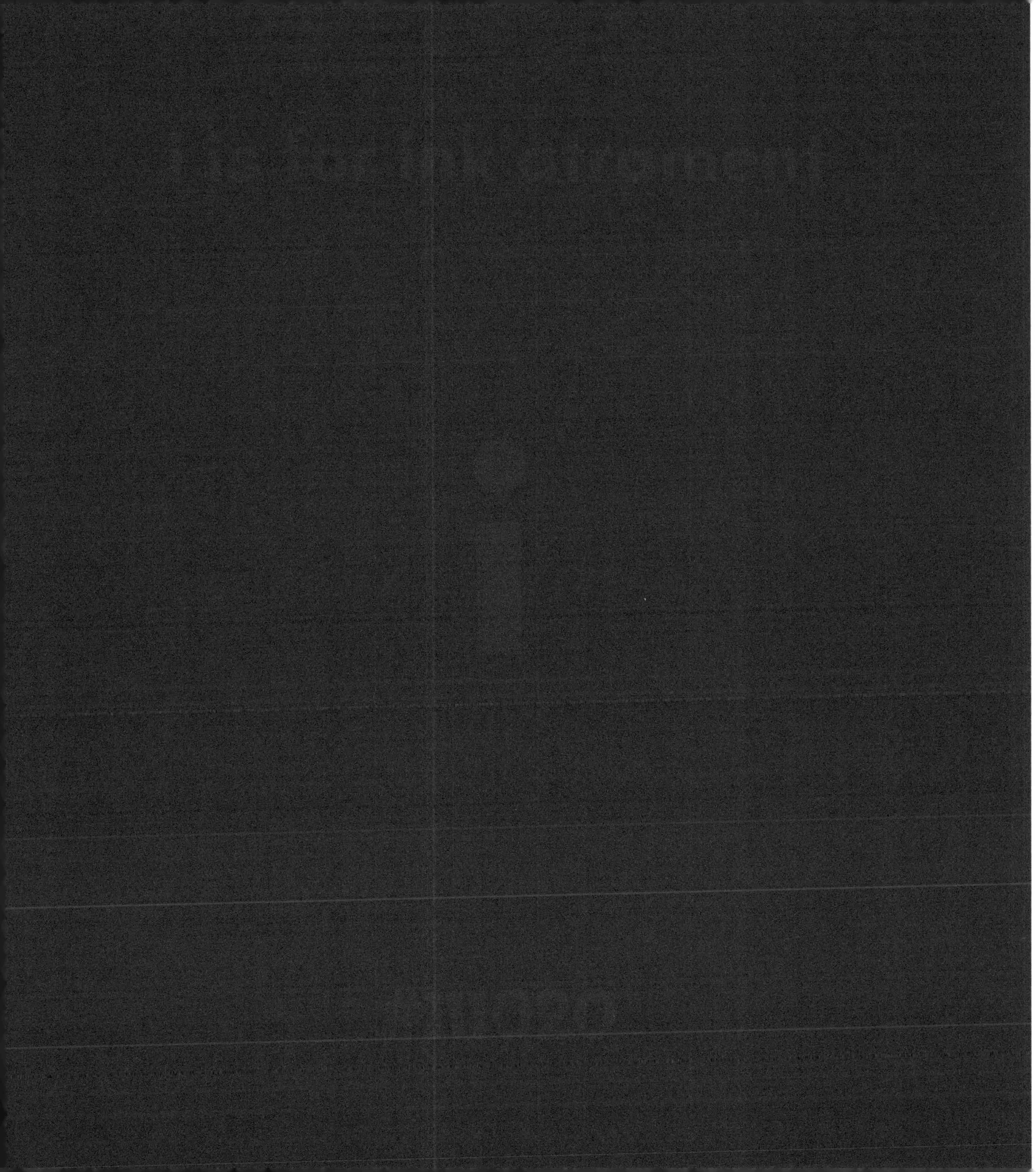

m is for mesosphere

m

41c 2022

N is for navy black

#263032

P is for peppercorn

P

#291F21

p is for personal

#2E3538

Q is for quarterback

q is for quartz 3

q

#272226

S is for shark

S

#25272C

s is for soot

s

#100C08

T

t is for tuatara

#363534

U is for universal black

#343434

u is for urban jungle

#aaaaaa

V is for vampire black

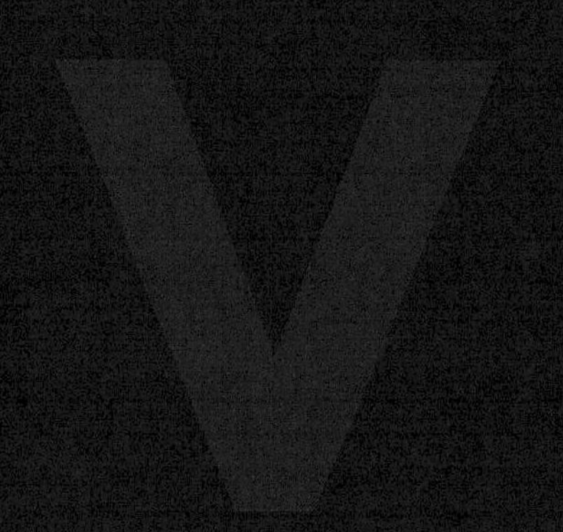

#080808

v is for vulcan

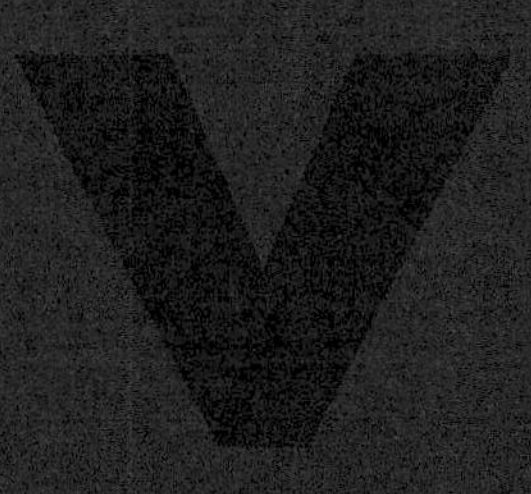

#101221

W is for wine trail

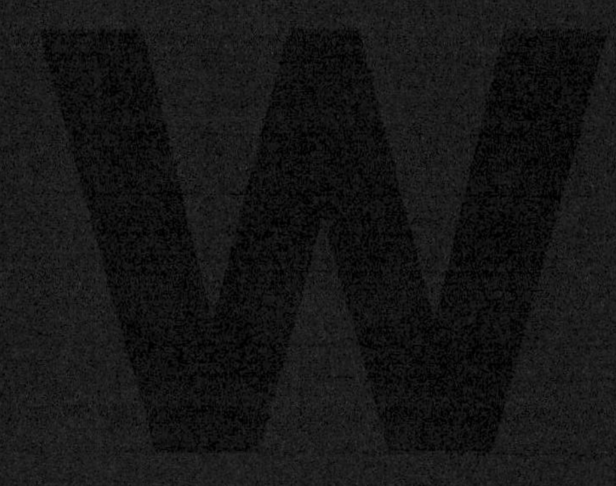

#27292D

w is for woodsmoke

W

#OCODOF

X is for xl black